6/67 Gumdrop Book

Pet Pals

Pet Cats

Julia Barnes

GARETH**STEVENS**
GS
PUBLISHING
A Member of the WRC Media Family of Companies

Please visit our web site at: www.garethstevens.com
For a free color catalog describing Gareth Stevens Publishing's
list of high-quality books and multimedia programs, call
1-800-542-2595.

Library of Congress Cataloging-in-Publication Data

Barnes, Julia, 1955-
    Pet cats / Julia Barnes. — North American ed.
      p. cm. — (Pet pals)
    Includes bibliographical references and index.
    ISBN-10: 0-8368-6776-9
    ISBN-13: 978-0-8368-6776-3 (lib. bdg.)
    1. Cats—Juvenile literature. I. Title.
    SF445.7.B377   2007
    636.8—dc22   2006042377

This edition first published in 2007 by
Gareth Stevens Publishing
A Weekly Reader Company
200 First Stamford Place
Stamford, CT 06912 USA

This U.S. edition copyright © 2007 by Gareth Stevens, Inc.
Original edition copyright © 2007 by Westline Publishing,
P.O. Box 8, Lydney, Gloucestershire, GL15 6YD, United Kingdom.

Gareth Stevens series editor: Leifa Butrick
Gareth Stevens cover design: Dave Kowalski
Gareth Stevens art direction: Tammy West

Picture Credits:
COREL, cover; Oxford Scientific, p. 5 (Richard Packwood).
All other images copyright © 2007, by Westline Publishing.

Printed in the United States of America

2 3 4 5 6 7 8 9 10 09 08 07

Cover Image: Cats like to be cuddled — but only when it suits them.

Contents

Words that appear in the glossary are printed in **boldface**
the first time they occur in the text.

The Wild Side

The mighty lion, the king of the beasts, is related to the cats that live with people today.

Meat-eating hunters that roamed the earth forty million years ago developed in different ways, depending on where they lived and what foods they could find.

The first true cat was among the animals that developed. It was called *Pseudaelarus*. The size of a cougar, it lived in North America and Europe twenty million years ago.

Out of Africa

The cat family later spread to Africa and Asia. Today, the cat family contains three groups:

- *Panthera*: big cats, such as lions and tigers
- *Acinonyx*: cats such as cheetahs that cannot **retract** their claws
- *Felis*: smaller cats, such as lynx or ocelots

A lion is a big cat.

African wildcats, which are part of the *felis* group, are the **ancestors** of modern **domestic cats**. African wildcats look and behave like domestic cats.

Some cats, such as lions, rely on teamwork when hunting, but African wildcats mainly hunt **rodents** and birds, which are small enough to catch without help. A wildcat creeps up on its **prey**, scarcely making a sound, advancing step by step. With a spring or a sudden burst of speed, it goes in for the kill. A bird or a rat is too small a meal to share, so an African wildcat lives and hunts alone.

This cat is an African wildcat, but it could easily be mistaken for a domestic cat.

Domestic Cats

Although dogs have lived with people for more than fourteen thousand years, cats have been people's pets for just four thousand years. Because they have come in from the wild only "recently," cats behave much like their African ancestors.

Paw Mark

The word *feline* means "catlike" or belonging to the cat family. It describes all members of the cat family, from lions and tigers to domestic cats.

The Human Link

The cat is a good mouse-catcher, so people welcomed cats into their homes.

In Egypt, pictures of cats date back to 2000 B.C. These pictures are the earliest records of domestic cats.

Cats first joined people when the Egyptians began to grow crops for food. After good **harvests**, people stored grain in barns so they would have enough to eat if future crops failed. Mice and rats, however, created a problem. They raided the grain stores, and the Egyptians saw their food supplies vanish before their eyes. One day, someone spotted a wild cat sneaking up on a mouse and catching it. That was the solution to the problem! Cats became the official mouse-catchers of Egypt.

Changing Fortunes

The cat's fame as a mouse-catcher spread, and people in many countries and of many different religions honored cats as holy animals. Because people believed cats had special powers, they looked after them.

Cats were worshipped as holy animals in Ancient Egypt.

Lucky or unlucky, this white cat looks very content on its satin sheets.

In **medieval** times, people still thought cats were powerful, but they grew suspicious of them. People linked cats with **witchcraft** and feared that evil spirits might live within cats' bodies. Many cats were killed. Cats did not become favorite pets again until the eighteenth century.

Paw Mark

The Egyptians valued cats so highly that they worshipped them. When a cat died, all the members of the family shaved off their eyebrows as a sign of respect. If someone killed a cat, that person was sentenced to death.

Lucky Cats

Today people have many different beliefs about cats.

- In North America, some people believe it is unlucky to see black cats because evil spirits live in the bodies of black cats.
- In the United Kingdom, the opposite is true. There, seeing a black cat is considered lucky because it means the person has passed by evil and has not been harmed.
- Japanese store owners often keep a small statue as a good luck charm of a white cat with one paw raised .
- The French believe that treating a cat well brings good luck to its owners.

Perfect Pets

Cats are the world's most popular pets. Seventy million cats live in homes in the United States.

Beauty, brains, agility — cats have them all. They are affectionate with their owners, but they also let their owners know that they are partly wild animals that do not need people. This mixture of tame and wild makes cats fascinating pets.

First Choice

Cats are admirable for many reasons, but what makes cats perfect pets?

- Cats are not expensive to buy unless people want **purebred** cats. Kittens are often free.
- It does not cost much to keep cats, and they are easy to look after.
- Cats do not need to be taken for walks.
- Cats do not need as much human company as dogs, so they suit people who are away from home all day.

A cat likes its people, but it also likes to please itself.

- Time spent with cats is very rewarding. Stroking cats and caring for them can even keep people healthier than they would be without their cats.
- Cats will live happily in a house or an apartment. Cats can even be happy without going outdoors, which means people who live on busy streets or have no backyards can still keep cats.

Feline Needs

Cats may be easy to take care of, but, like all animals, they have needs that owners should know about.

- Cats need the correct type of food.
- They need up-to-date **vaccinations** and other health care.
- When owners go away for more than a day, they need to get someone to take care of their cats.
- Long-haired cats need grooming.
- **House cats** need activity to make up for not going outdoors.

Allergy Alert

Some people are **allergic** to cats and may suffer from skin problems, breathing problems, or watery eyes if a cat is kept in the house. Doctors can test people for this type of allergy.

Cats are happy living in warm and comfortable family homes where they get plenty of food.

A Cat's Body

Cat owners should understand how their pets' bodies work.

Eyes

Although a cat can see what is ahead of it very well, it cannot see anything behind it unless it turns its head. It has excellent night vision, so it can hunt in the dark.

Nose

A cat's sense of smell is thirty times better than a human's.

Tongue

A cat uses its rough tongue for grooming. When a cat drinks water, its tongue becomes spoon-shaped and flicks the water back into its mouth.

Teeth

Cats have thirty teeth, two fewer than people. Each cat has sixteen teeth in the upper jaw and fourteen in the lower jaw.

Whiskers

The length of a cat's whiskers is equal to the width of its body. A cat uses its whiskers to decide if it can get through an opening.

Tail

A cat uses its tail to help it balance when it is walking on a narrow ledge. A cat uses its tail the same way a tightrope walker uses a pole.

Ears

With thirty muscles in each ear, a cat can turn its ears very quickly toward any sound it hears.

Coat

Some cats are long-haired, and some are short-haired. Some purebred cats have unusual coats. The Rex cat has a wavy coat.

Body

With its very **flexible** body, a cat can put itself into many different positions. It can arch its back, sleep in a circle, or twist around to reach its tail.

Paws

A cat will investigate a new object with its front paws. A hunting cat will touch its prey with a paw to see if it is dead or alive.

Claws

Retractable claws are important to a cat. It pushes its claws out when it wants to use them for scratching, climbing, or fighting. It pulls them back in when it does not need them.

Purebred Cats

Long-haired, short-haired, or even curly-haired — cats come in many varieties.

Some people want purebred kittens, so they find breeders who specialize in certain cat breeds. The advantage of buying a purebred cat is that people know what it will look like as an adult and what kind of personality it will have.

Persian
Of all purebred cats, Persians are the most popular. They have long hair, chunky bodies, and flattened faces. Under all the fur, they have sleek, slim bodies. Persians come in many colors. Peke-faced Persians have upturned noses like Pekingese dogs. Persians are laid-back and love people. They are ideal choices for people who want house cats.

Siamese
These beautiful cats are famous for their dazzling blue eyes. The first Siamese were Sealpoints, with cream-colored bodies and dark brown faces, ears, legs, and tails. They originally came from Thailand, once known as Siam. Siamese cats have loud voices and often sound like babies crying. Siamese are intelligent and curious cats, but they demand a lot of attention.

Maine Coon

This all-American breed was developed in the state of Maine about one hundred years ago. Maine Coons have long, rugged coats to protect them from cold weather and large, muscular bodies. A Maine Coon can weigh 18 pounds (8 kilograms) without being overweight. These tough outdoor cats enjoy being part of families.

Abyssinian

Abyssinian cats look like the cats of Ancient Egypt, and they may well have links that go back to ancient times. They have lean bodies; elegant, arched necks; and large, pointed ears. Abyssinians are intelligent and friendly but not as demanding as Siamese cats.

Rex

Unlike other breeds, all varieties of Rex cats have naturally curly hair. The coats of long-haired Selkirk Rex cats fall in soft, loose curls. The Cornish Rex in the picture has long, crinkly whiskers to go with its wavy coat. Rex cats are lively, intelligent, and good-humored.

Anything Goes

Purebred cats are beautiful, but most pet owners prefer ordinary cats.

Pet stores sell cats of mixed breeding; animal shelters give them away. People who own cats sometimes have kittens to give away.

Cats of mixed breeding come in many sizes, shapes, and colors. Everyone has a favorite, whether it is long-haired or short-haired, tabby or tortoiseshell. A cat's color and markings make it unique.

Tabby

The original wild cat color was made up of black hairs topped with yellow, which is known as agouti. This basic color developed into a pattern of spots and stripes against a paler background. It is called the tabby pattern, and it is so common that some people think the pattern is a breed of cat and not just a marking.

Tabby markings help this hunting cat blend into the under-growth. Its prey will not see it hiding among the leaves.

Tortoiseshell

Cats that have three colors in their coats — black, orange, and cream — are called tortoiseshell. If a cat also has white patches, it is called tortie and white, or calico. Most tortoiseshell cats are females.

White

One of the oldest colors for domestic cats is white. It often goes with gold eyes or eyes of two different colors, known as odd eyes. Many times, white cats that have blue eyes are deaf.

Black

Many people in the United States think black cats are unlucky, but black cats are popular in other countries.

Orange

Orange, or ginger-colored, cats come in dark and light shades, and they often have tabby markings. Many famous cats were ginger cats: Thomasina in the book and movie, Morris the fussy eater, and Spot, Data's pet cat in *Star Trek: The Next Generation*.

Tortoiseshell cats are an interesting blend of colors.

Paw Mark

Cats of mixed breeding are generally hardy, healthy animals and are easier to care for than purebred cats.

This ginger cat has tabby markings.

Feline Lifestyles

House cats and indoor/outdoor cats lead different lives, but most of their needs are the same.

People want their cats to be safe, but they also want to make sure their cats have interesting lives. Usually they choose one of two lifestyles for their cats.

A cat that spends part of the day outside will climb, hunt, and explore.

Indoor/Outdoor Cat

The most natural way to keep a cat is to let it divide its time between living in the house and spending time outdoors. It will enjoy being in a warm, comfortable home, but it will also have the chance to go free, investigating new sights and scents.

An indoor/outdoor cat has some special requirements.
- Its owner's house should not be on a busy street where the cat could be hurt in traffic.
- Its owner must be willing to let it in or out frequently, or else its owner needs to provide a cat-flap (a cat-sized door) on an outside door.

- Its owner should expect that the cat will be a hunter and will chase birds and small animals.

House Cat

People who live in an apartment and have no backyard, or who worry that their cats may be hurt in traffic, often keep their cats indoors all the time. Most cats adapt well to indoor life, but there can be problems.

- An older cat that is used to going outdoors will not like being kept indoors all the time. A kitten is much more likely to be happy with an indoor lifestyle if it has never known anything else.
- A house cat will not be able to cope with the outside world because it has not learned how. Owners must make sure their homes are secure so their house cats cannot escape and get into trouble.
- A house cat needs to exercise its brains and its body. Its owner must supply toys and set aside time for play sessions.
- A house cat still needs to scratch, so it should have a scratching post, or the house will soon be in ruins!

A house cat will be content if it has never known an outdoor life.

Getting Ready

Cats do not need much equipment, but here are a few items to buy if you decide to get a cat.

Food
Find out what your cat has been eating and have a supply of food ready for its arrival.

Bowls
A cat needs two bowls — one for food and one for water. The stainless steel type is sturdy and easy to clean.

Scratching Post
All cats and kittens scratch to sharpen their claws. If owners do not provide scratching posts, their furniture and curtains will suffer. A house cat should have a "cat tree," with at least two columns of scratching posts, as well as tunnels, nests, and perches.

Paw Mark
A cat will be happy with a cardboard box, lined with some soft material, for a bed. It does not need a fancy, expensive cat bed.

A scratching post gives a cat an opportunity to climb and to sharpen its claws.

Litter Box

A **litter** box for the cat's waste is a must for a house cat. Litter boxes are also good for cats that can go outdoors so that they don't have accidents in the house. The box should be 3 to 4 inches (7.5 to 10 centimeters) deep and be filled with cat litter. Keep the litter box in one place, such as the kitchen, so your cat will know where to find it.

Collar

Collars are useful for cats that go outdoors because they can carry some form of identification. A microchip, implanted under a cat's skin, however, is a permanent form of ID.

Toys

Cats are very playful animals. They will have fun with any toys you give them. A feather attached to a simple piece of string can provide hours of fun.

Bed

A cat is an expert at finding cozy places to sleep, but it will also like having its own special bed. Cat beds are available in all shapes and sizes, ranging from beanbags to hammock-type beds that fit over radiators.

Cat Carrier

You will need a carrier to take your cat to a veterinarian or to a **kennel** if you decide to board the cat when you go away for more than a day. You can also use the carrier to keep your cat safe for a short time when you introduce other pets in the family to the cat.

Lining a cat carrier with soft blankets helps a cat get used to the carrier.

The Right Choice

When everything is ready, it is time to choose a cat.

You may get a cat from a breeder, a pet store, an animal shelter, or a friend, but, in all cases, you need to look at it carefully to be sure that the cat is healthy. If you get a kitten, it must be at least seven weeks old before leaving its mother.

Male or Female

Male and female cats both make wonderful pets. Males will grow bigger than females, but every cat is different as far as personality is concerned. Ask the breeder or cat expert to pick out the males and females so you know which one you have.

If you do not plan to breed cats, your cat will need **neutering**. Take your veterinarian's advice on the best age for neutering.

Indoor cats appreciate the company of another cat.

Paw Mark

A male cat is called a **tom cat**. A female cat is known as a **queen**.

Signs of Good Health

Be sure the cat you choose is healthy.

Ears
Check to see if the cat's ears are clean and have no bad odor. Dark gray dirt in its ears could indicate ear mites.

Eyes
Look for clean, bright eyes.

Nose
There should be no sign of crustiness or discharge.

Mouth
Open the cat's mouth. The gums should be pink, the teeth should be clean, and the cat should not have bad breath.

Body
A cat should not be too fat or too thin.

Paws
Lift up the cat's paws to be sure no cracks or cuts are visible on the pads of its feet.

Coat
The cat's coat should be clean, with no black flecks of dirt, which could indicate fleas.

Tail
Dirt or matting around the base of the cat's tail could mean the cat is suffering from diarrhea.

More than One

Wild cats lived alone, so an indoor/outdoor cat will be perfectly happy on its own. A house cat that does not go outdoors, however, will find life more interesting if it has another cat to play with. Kittens that grow up together will remain friends throughout their lives, and you will have a lot of fun watching them play together.

Making Friends

Everything will seem very strange to a cat when it first arrives in its new home.

Cats are curious animals and love to investigate anything that is new to them. When it first arrives in a home, a new pet may be a little nervous, but it will still want to explore.

Cats like to be cuddled — but only when it suits them.

Early Days

Let your cat get used to its new home a room at a time. To begin with, let it have the run of the kitchen or whichever room you have decided should be the cat's base. This base should be the room where the cat is fed, where you place its litter box, and where it has a cozy bed. When your cat becomes more confident, it can explore the rest of the house.

Meeting the Family

Cats like people. They love to lie on laps and be stroked and cuddled. A cat, however, will decide when it wants someone's company! Remember the following points:

- Do not pick up or carry your new cat. It might scratch you.

- Do not handle a new pet too much. A cat needs a chance to get used to its new surroundings.
- To begin with, play with your cat on the floor. Choose a game, such as playing with a ball on a string. The cat will soon join in.
- Do not disturb your cat when it is eating, sleeping, or using its litter box.
- Always be gentle with your cat. Stroke it the way its hair lies and avoid sudden movements.

Other Pets

Cats and dogs do not have to be enemies. If you also have a dog, take care during its first few meetings with the cat. Start with the cat in a carrier and allow both animals to take a look at each other. Then, let the cat out of the carrier, but keep the dog on a leash. When the dog is calm around the cat, you can let it off the leash.

Never forget that a cat has a very strong **hunting instinct** and must be kept away from smaller pets. The cat will kill them if it has a chance.

If a dog learns not to chase, and a cat knows the dog is trustworthy, they will live together very happily.

Paw Mark

Cats love to investigate household equipment such as washing machines and dryers. Make sure the doors to these appliances are closed at all times to avoid accidents.

Cat Care

A person who takes care of a cat becomes its special friend.

Cat owners need to play with their cats to keep the cats happy, but they have other **responsibilities** as well.

Cats help each other keep clean. Grooming each other is also a way to make friends.

Feeding

Most adult cats need to eat twice a day. Growing kittens need three or four small meals a day. Cats soon learn who in the family provides the food. Your cat will think of you as its special friend if you give it at least one of its meals every day. In order to stay healthy, cats need a diet that has the correct balance of **nutrients**. Packaged food that is specially made for cats is much better than table scraps. Veterinarians are a good source of advice on what to feed cats.

Health Care

All cats need to be wormed, to have flea treatments, and to be vaccinated against infectious diseases. A veterinarian can give good advice on all the health care a cat needs.

Grooming

Cats are very clean animals and will groom themselves. Short-haired cats do not need any help, but long-haired cats get mats and tangles if their owners do not comb them. If an owner starts combing a long-haired cat when it is young, the cat will learn to sit still.

To Hunt or Not to Hunt?

House cats do not have a chance to hunt, but pet cats that are allowed outdoors will do their best to catch birds and mice. Some cats like to eat their prey, but the cats may get **parasites**, such as worms when they do. Other cats lose interest in their prey as soon as the hunt is over. Owners who want their cats to be less successful as hunters should try the following:

- Putting a collar with a bell on a cat prevents the cat from creeping up silently on animals. Some "anti-hunt" collars make noise when the cats wearing them jump up.
- Cats like to hunt at dawn and at dusk. Keeping a cat in the house at

A cat will make up its own hunting games. This cat is ready to spring out of a paper bag.

these times will cut down on its hunting.
- Playing hunting games with a cat, such as letting it creep up on a toy and pounce on it, gives the cat a chance to use its hunting instinct without doing any harm.

Paw Mark

Cats should have water to drink rather than milk. Cats like milk, but it is bad for them and can lead to stomach upsets.

Cat Behavior

Cats are secretive animals. It is not always easy to figure out how their minds work.

Cats need to let other cats know how they are feeling. If you learn to read the signs, you, too, will know what mood your cat is in.

Cat Calls

Cats make many sounds, and each sound means something.

Purring: This sound is like an engine running. It usually shows that a cat is contented, but sometimes a cat will purr if it is approached by a stranger or when it is in pain. That kind of purring means "I am friendly and ready to be stroked" or "Please help me."

Meowing: This sound is a cat's way of getting attention. It can mean anything from "hello" to "feed me."

Hissing and Spitting: When a cat hisses or spits, it is angry and is trying to act fierce.

Growling: Cats make a low, rumbling sound as a warning, especially when they are telling another cat to go away.

Caterwauling: The loud howls or screeches made by male cats fighting over their territories is called caterwauling. This alarming sound is usually heard at night.

Paw Mark

Cats greet each other by rubbing faces. If your cat greets you by standing on its hind legs, it may be trying to reach your face.

Body Movement

A cat's movements also give clues to how it is feeling.

Happy Cat: When its body is upright and its tail is held high, a cat is happy. It often holds its ears forward. If a cat is relaxed, it may half-close its eyes. A long, slow blink with both eyes is a sign of friendship. If your cat blinks at you, it expects you to blink back.

Hunting Cat: A tense, alert cat, crouching low on the ground with its tail held down, is hunting.

Scared Cat: A cat that is worried will be on the alert, twitching its ears to pick up sounds. If it becomes frightened, it will arch its back, and the hair on its back will stand on end. The cat is trying to look big and threatening.

Angry Cat: When a cat flicks its tail from side to side, it is angry. It may flatten its ears, bare its teeth, and spit.

A hunting cat stands still and silent so it does not disturb its prey.

Training Targets

Going step by step and finding just the right treat are the secrets to training a cat.

Although cats like to please themselves, they can also be trained to do a number of tricks. Owners must be patient and find tasty treats that cats think are worth working for. Some cat treats come in cat-sized bites. These kinds of treats are good because a cat will eat one quickly and be ready to earn more.

Clicker Training

A clicker can speed up training. A clicker is a small box with a metal tongue that makes a clicking sound when someone presses it. To a cat, the click means "Yes, that is right. Now you get a reward." All the trainer needs to do is to click and then reward the cat with a treat.

After a few practice sessions, a cat can learn to respond to the sound of a clicker and come when it is called.

Easy Tricks

Here are some simple tricks for training a cat. Remember to be patient. Your cat will learn.

Come

- Stroke your cat so you have its attention. Then step back a couple of paces.
- Call "Come, kitty" and show the cat you have a treat. The moment the cat starts to move toward you, click. Reward it with the treat when the cat has reached you.
- Repeat this exercise for a few days, gradually putting more space between you and the cat. In time, the cat will learn the command. You can then try calling your cat from room to room or even call the cat to come in from your backyard.

Beg

- Show your cat that you have a tasty treat.
- Hold the treat above the cat's nose, high enough so that it cannot stretch up to reach it.
- When your cat cannot get the treat, it will use its paws to try to grab the treat. As soon as

You can teach your cat to sit up and beg for a treat.

your cat lifts its front paws, click and reward.
- Next time, wait a little longer before you click and reward so your cat will get used to balancing.
- When your cat learns how to "beg" for its treat, introduce the command "Beg."

Invent Your Own Tricks

Another easy trick is a High Five, where your cat pats the palm of your hand. For a rollover, use a treat to encourage the cat to follow your hand until the cat rolls over onto its back.

Glossary

allergic: likely to have a reaction, such as a runny nose or a skin rash, to cat hair or other substances

ancestors: relatives from the distant past

domestic cats: cats that no longer live in the wild

feline: catlike or belonging to the cat family

feral: domestic cats that live in the wild

flexible: able to bend and move smoothly and easily

harvests: crops that are gathered after they have ripened

house cats: cats that live indoors and never go outdoors

hunting instinct: the natural drive to hunt

kennel: a place where cats are looked after when their owners are away

litter: material used to absorb wastes from a cat's body

medieval: a time in the past, from 900 A.D. to 1500 A.D.

neutering: surgery that prevents an animal from reproducing

nutrients: substances in food that keep an animal healthy

parasites: plants or animals living in or on other plants or animals

prey: creatures killed by a hunting animal

purebred: describing an animal produced by a male and female of the same recognized breed; for example, both parents are Siamese

queen: a female cat

responsibilities: jobs a person has promised to do

retract: to pull in claws whenever the animal does not need them

rodents: small animals that gnaw with their front teeth, such as mice and rats

tom cat: a male cat

vaccinations: injections to protect cats against diseases

witchcraft: the practice of magic associated with witches

More Books to Read

101 Facts About Kittens
Claire Horton-Bussey
Gareth Stevens

Cat
Juliet Clutton-Brock
DK Publishing

How to Talk to Your Cat
Jean Craighead George
HarperCollins

Meow! A Guide to Understanding Your Cat
Caroline Heens
Kingfisher Books

Totally Fun Things to Do with Your Cat
Maxine Rock
John Wiley and Sons

Web Sites

Cats Just for Kids
www.americanhumane.org/kids/cats.htm

Kitties for Kiddies
dnscs.com/kfk/

The Swiss Cat Site
mypage.bluewin.ch/katzenseite/docs/en/games/memory_js/
memory_js.html

Note to educators and parents: The publisher has carefully reviewed these Web sites to ensure that they are suitable for children. Many Web sites change frequently, however, and Gareth Stevens, Inc., cannot guarantee that a site's future contents will continue to meet our high standards of quality and educational value. Be advised that children should be closely supervised whenever they access the Internet.

Index